Being Trustworthy

A Book About Trustworthiness

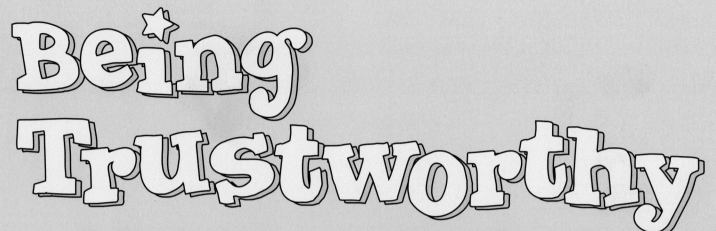

by Mary Small   illustrated by Stacey Previn

PICTURE WINDOW BOOKS
Minneapolis, Minnesota

Thanks to our advisors for their expertise, research, and advice:

Bambi L. Wagner, Director of Education
Institute for Character Development, Des Moines, Iowa
National Faculty Member/ Trainer,
Josephson Institute of Ethics - CHARACTER COUNTS!℠
Los Angeles, California

Susan Kesselring, M.A., Literacy Educator
Rosemount-Apple Valley-Egan (Minnesota) School District

Editorial Director: Carol Jones
Managing Editor: Catherine Neitge
Creative Director: Keith Griffin
Editor: Jacqueline A. Wolfe
Story Consultant: Terry Flaherty
Designer: Joe Anderson
Page Production: Picture Window Books
The illustrations in this book were created with acrylics.

Picture Window Books
5115 Excelsior Boulevard
Suite 232
Minneapolis, MN 55416
877-845-8392
www.picturewindowbooks.com

Printed in the United States of America.

Library of Congress Cataloging-in-Publication Data
Small, Mary.
Being trustworthy / by Mary Small ; illustrated by Stacey Previn.
p. cm. – (Way to be!)
Includes bibliographical references and index.
ISBN 1-4048-1054-4 (hard cover)
1. Trust–Juvenile literature.
2. Reliability–Juvenile literature. I. Previn, Stacey. II. Title. III. Series.
BJ1500.T78S63 2006
179'.9–dc22   2005004276

Do people trust you?

Are you trustworthy? When you are trustworthy, people can count on you to do the right thing. Being trustworthy sometimes takes courage. It isn't always easy. But it is worth the work to have people trust you.

There are lots of ways to show you are trustworthy.

In school, the students are sure to keep their eyes on their own test.

They are being trustworthy.

Jeremy takes the trash out when it is his turn. His parents can rely on him.

He is being trustworthy.

Sally watches Amber's bike for her while Amber is in the store.

She is being trustworthy.

Greg goes to the store for his dad and is sure to give him back all of the change.

He is being trustworthy.

Paul points out to Mrs. Baker that money fell out of her purse.

He is being trustworthy.

Brian keeps an eye on his baby sister
even when his friends are over visiting.

He is being trustworthy.

Heather doesn't touch the checkers game even though Billy isn't watching her.

She is being trustworthy.

Candace comes home exactly when she said she'd be there.

She is being trustworthy.

Matthew keeps his mom's birthday surprise a secret.

He is being trustworthy.

Matthew walks the puppy for his mom like he promised, even when the weather is bad.

He is being trustworthy.

At the Library

Blair, Eric. *The Boy Who Cried Wolf*. Minneapolis: Picture Window Books, 2004.

Loewen, Nancy. *How Could You? : Kids Talk About Trust*. Minneapolis: Picture Window Books, 2003.

McKissack, Patricia C. *The Honest-to-Goodness Truth*. New York: Antheum, 2000.

On the Web

FactHound offers a safe, fun way to find Web sites related to this book.

All of the sites on FactHound have been researched by our staff.

www.facthound.com

1. Visit the FactHound home page.
2. Enter a search word related to this book, or type in this special code: 1404810544
3. Click the FETCH IT button.

Your trusty FactHound will fetch the best Web sites for you!

Index

mom, 21

money, 10, 13

puppy, 22

sister, 14

store, 8, 10

surprise, 21

test, 4